DATE DUE

Muscles

Injury, Illness and Health

Carol Ballard

Heinemann Library
Chicago, Illinois

© 2003 Heinemann Library
a division of Reed Elsevier Inc.
Chicago, Illinois

Customer Service 888-454-2279

Visit our website at www.heinemannlibrary.com

Design: Jo Hinton-Malivoire and AMR
Illustrations: Art Construction

Originated by Blenheim Colour Ltd
Printed in China by Wing King Tong

07 06 05 04 03
10 9 8 7 6 5 4 3 2

Library of Congress Cataloging-in-Publication Data
Ballard, Carol.
  Muscles / Carol Ballard.
    v. cm. -- (Body focus)
Includes bibliographical references and index.
Contents: Different muscles -- Healthy muscles --
Exercise and muscle -- Skeletal muscles -- Inside a
muscle -- Attachments of muscles -- Working muscles --
When a muscle contracts -- Athletes' muscles --
Bodybuilding -- Muscle problems -- Muscles of the face
and head -- Chest muscles -- Heart muscles --
Abdominal muscles.
  ISBN: 1-4034-0752-5 (HC), 1-4034-3300-3 (Pbk.)
  1. Muscles--Juvenile literature. [1. Muscles.] I. Title. II.
Series.
  QP321 .B27 2003
  612.7'4--dc21

2002152974

Acknowledgments
The author and publishers are grateful to the following for permission to reproduce
copyright material:
p. 7 (left) SPL/Astrid and Hans Frieder Michler; p. 7 (right) Trip/M. Walker; pp. 8, 9 Corbis/Royalty Free; p. 10 Corbis/Ed Bock/The Stock Market; p. 11 NASA; p. 14 SPL/Manfred Kage; pp. 22, 24, 25, 27, 33, 41 Getty Images; p. 23 Philippe Plailly/Eurelios/Imagingbody; p. 31 Corbis/Robbie Jack; p. 32 SPL/Quest; p. 39 SPL/Damien Lovegrove; p. 42 SPL/Philippe Plailly; p. 43 Corbis.

The cover image of the colored SPECT scan of a human heart appears courtesy of Science Photo Library/ISM.

The publisher would like to thank David Wright and Kelley Staley for their assistance with the preparation of this book.

Every effort has been made to contact copyright holders of any material reproduced in this book. Any omissions will be rectified in subsequent printings if notice is given to the publisher.

Some words are shown in bold, **like this.** You can find out what they mean by looking in the glossary.

CONTENTS

INTRODUCTION

Muscles are vital to the human body. They carry out essential functions and allow you to move all or part of your body. Muscles make up 40 to 50 percent of the body weight of an average adult man and 30 to 40 percent of that of a woman.

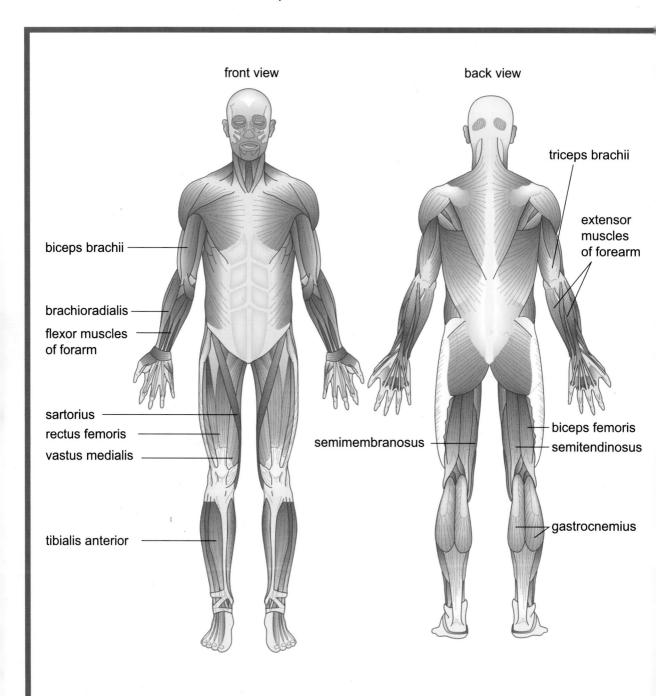

front view

back view

biceps brachii

brachioradialis

flexor muscles of forarm

sartorius

rectus femoris

vastus medialis

tibialis anterior

triceps brachii

extensor muscles of forearm

semimembranosus

biceps femoris

semitendinosus

gastrocnemius

These pictures show the main muscles in the body that allow you to move and maintain posture.

Did you know you have more than 600 muscles in your body?

When you think about muscles, you probably think first about those that allow you to move. Most are attached to bones, and their contractions pull the bones into new positions. Some muscles, such as certain muscles in the face, are not attached to bones. Instead, they move skin, allowing you to move your lips and change your facial expressions. Muscles in your throat move the vocal cords, allowing you to talk, sing, and shout.

sartorius   gluteus

Different muscles are responsible for different types of movement. The strong muscles of the thigh and buttock help move the whole body. Tiny muscles attached to the eyes make very small, precise movements.

Muscles are also responsible for maintaining body position. By controlling the positions of the bones and joints, muscles help the body keep a balanced posture, which is particularly important for sports such as gymnastics and ice-skating.

The heart is one of your most important muscles. It beats continuously, pumping blood to every part of the body. Muscles in the chest move the rib cage, allowing you to breathe in and out.

The digestive system has muscles throughout its length, which help push food along. Other internal organs and vessels, such as blood vessels, also have muscles.

Muscles that you use to move all or part of your body are under your control. You can decide whether or not to kick a ball, raise your hand, or nod your head. Other muscles, such as the heart muscle and those in the digestive system, operate without your having to think about it at all. *I'll explain that in the second part*

When muscles work, they use energy and release heat. This helps keep the body warm.

Keeping muscles healthy
Food is important in helping to keep muscles strong and healthy. It makes sense to try to eat a balanced diet that contains all the **nutrients** your muscles need to grow and develop. Exercise is important, too. The more you use your muscles, the stronger they will become.

DIFFERENT TYPES OF MUSCLES

Muscles vary in size, shape, and internal structure, depending on their function and position within the body. Each is specially designed to carry out its function.

Voluntary and involuntary muscles

Some actions, such as moving your hand, walking, and turning your head, are all under your control. You can choose whether or not to make these movements. Muscles involved in movements of this sort are called **voluntary muscles**. Other movements happen without having to think about them. Your heart continues to beat, whether you are awake or asleep. And the muscles in your digestive system push food along continuously. You cannot control the actions of these muscles, and as a result, they are called **involuntary muscles**.

Skeletal muscle

As its name suggests, the main function of a skeletal muscle is to move bones. It is also called **striated** muscle because, if you look at it under a microscope, you can see it has a pattern of stripes, or striations. Most skeletal muscles are voluntary muscles, but they can sometimes also act without your control. This happens when you experience a muscle twitch.

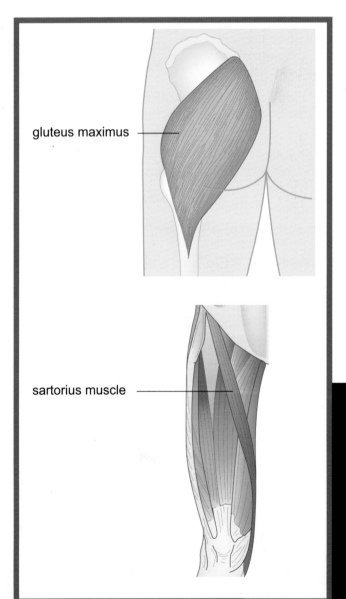

gluteus maximus

sartorius muscle

Skeletal muscles come in a wide variety of shapes and sizes. The longest muscle in the human body is the sartorius, at the front of the thigh. The strongest muscle is the gluteus maximus, responsible for moving the hip and thigh. It is used when powerful movements are needed, as in climbing stairs, running, and jumping.

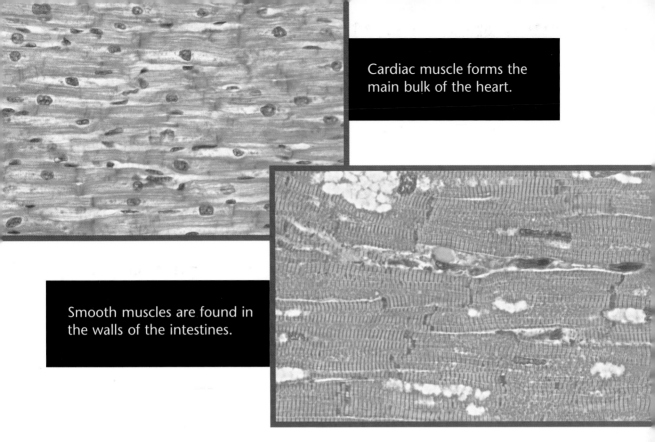

Cardiac muscle forms the main bulk of the heart.

Smooth muscles are found in the walls of the intestines.

Cardiac muscle

Cardiac muscle is found only in the heart. Under a microscope, you can see that it has a striped pattern, similar to that of skeletal muscle. Cardiac muscle is an involuntary muscle. The speed at which it contracts is controlled by its own built-in pacemaker. It can also be influenced by some **hormones.**

Smooth muscle

The walls of some internal organs and vessels contain **smooth muscle.** This type of muscle also occurs in the skin, attached to hair cells. It does not have a striped pattern. Smooth muscle is an involuntary muscle, and causes movement inside internal organs and vessels.

Safety system

Muscles used in breathing are partly under your control. You can decide to hold your breath, and you can breathe more quickly or slowly on purpose. This could be dangerous, however, and so your body has a safety override system. If you are not taking in enough oxygen, your brain takes charge and makes you breathe normally again. When you breathe too quickly, you can take in too much oxygen and feel light-headed and dizzy. Again, your brain will usually take control and slow the breathing back to a normal rate.

HEALTHY MUSCLES

✴ Keeping your muscles strong and healthy helps you get the most out of everything that you do. The food you eat and the exercise you do both have an effect on your muscles. Muscles can be easily damaged, so exercise safely.

Food (muscles are fibrous tissues)

Muscle **fibers** are made up of **protein** molecules, which are made up of smaller molecules called **amino acids**. Your body cannot make amino acids. You have to get them from the food you eat. Good sources of protein include meat, fish, eggs, nuts, and legumes. You should try to eat some of these foods every day.

When muscles work, they use energy. This energy comes from food. Starchy foods, such as bread, rice, pasta, and bananas, are all full of energy. Long-distance runners often eat a pasta-rich meal the night before a race, so they have plenty of energy stored up for the next day. Fatty foods and sugary foods also provide energy, but they are not good for your health, so you should not eat too much of these.

Regular exercise, such as swimming, can help keep your muscles strong and healthy.

Vitamins and minerals

Vitamins and **minerals** are important for the health of every part of your body, including your muscles. Fresh fruit and vegetables provide all that you need. Bananas are especially good because they are rich in potassium, which is essential for muscle function.

Exercise

The more a muscle is used, the stronger it becomes. Muscles that are not used gradually shrink and become weak. Like the skeletal muscles, the **cardiac muscle** of the heart also benefits from exercise. Dancing, swimming, cycling, running, gymnastics, and ball games are all exercises that help keep your muscles strong and healthy. If you can do these types of exercises three times a week, you'll soon feel the benefit. It's a good idea to gradually build up the amount of exercise you do, rather than suddenly launching into a demanding exercise program. This gives your body time to adjust and become used to the extra work you are making it do.

When you exercise, you sweat. As you sweat, your body loses water and you can become dehydrated. Make sure you drink plenty of water when you exercise.

Remember to warm up gently before you begin strenuous exercise. This will help you avoid injuries to your muscles.

Avoiding injury

Before you exercise, your muscles are cold and stiff. They can be easily injured if you exercise vigorously without warming them up first. You should begin gently with slow movements. Your muscles will then warm up, and they will be less likely to become injured when you begin your activity.

After exercise, a few minutes of gentle stretches will help your muscles to cool down slowly. This can help prevent stiffness and soreness later.

EXERCISE AND MUSCLES

Exercising a muscle increases its size and strength. Different types of exercise affect different muscles in different ways. Exercise routines can be specifically designed to develop muscles in a particular part of the body, improve stamina, and increase suppleness or overall strength.

Interval training

During interval training, a short burst of high-intensity activity increases the heart rate. This is followed by a short recovery period, during which the heart rate slowly decreases. Another burst of high-intensity activity is followed by another recovery period, and this pattern is repeated throughout the training session. In a gym, a typical pattern might be 40 seconds of rowing as hard as you can, followed by a 20-second recovery period of sitting still. Interval training mimics the pattern of many sports. In tennis and racquetball, for example, players exert themselves fully while the ball is in play and then have a short recovery period between points.

When you exercise a muscle, it gets bigger and stronger. The muscle has no more muscle **fibers** than before you began exercising, but each individual muscle fiber becomes thicker. The blood supply to the muscle also increases, so more oxygen and energy can be brought to the muscle and more waste products can be carried away.

Aerobic exercise, such as dancing and jogging, helps to increase stamina. This allows you to continue exercising for longer periods. **Anaerobic** exercise, such as weightlifting, builds up muscle strength for short bursts of intense activity. Many people have an exercise routine of interval training, which alternates aerobic and anaerobic exercise to build both strength and stamina.

Muscles that are not used for a long time, for example, when a leg is in a cast, can shrink and become weak.

Overexercising

Too much exercise can damage muscles. Scientists have examined muscle tissue from athletes before and after vigorous exercise and have found tiny tears and other damage. The level of muscle **proteins** in the blood also increases after exercise, suggesting that they have been released from damaged muscle fibers.

Lack of exercise

Lack of exercise can cause atrophy, or shrinking, in muscles. People who have an arm or leg in a cast for a long time often find that when the cast is removed, the muscles are weak through lack of use. Muscle fibers are slowly replaced by fibrous connective tissue. This change cannot be reversed, but exercise can help increase the size and strength of the remaining muscle fibers. **Physical therapy** is often used to help people regain muscle strength after an injury or prolonged bed rest.

Astronauts need to exercise when they are in space to try to maintain their muscles' strength.

☀ Muscles in space

Astronauts who spend long periods of time in space find that their muscles slowly decrease in size. Although they exercise as much as possible, their muscles do not have to work as hard in space as they do on Earth, because they are not pulling against the force of gravity. The nerve endings of astronauts' muscles are also often damaged, which makes coordination and precise movements difficult.

SKELETAL MUSCLES

The human body contains more than 600 skeletal muscles. They differ in shape, size, and function. Muscles can be named and classified according to their shape, size, action, and location.

Strap muscles

These muscles, also called parallel muscles, are the simplest of the skeletal muscles and are not very strong. Bundles of muscle **fibers,** called **fascicles,** run parallel to each other along the length of the muscle. Some of the muscles in the abdominal wall are strap muscles.

Fusiform muscles

Fusiform muscles are thick in the middle and thin at each end. The fat middle section is made up of fascicles, which run parallel to each other along the length of the muscle. The thin end sections are strong **tendons,** which attach the muscle to the bone. The biceps muscle, attached to the shoulder blade and lower arm bones, is a fusiform muscle. When it contracts, the lower arm is raised.

Pennate muscles

Pennate muscles are made up of short fascicles. A tendon runs along the center of the fascicles, which spread out in a fan shape. There are several different arrangements of fascicles and tendons. In some muscles, such as those that move the thumb, fascicles are arranged along one side of the tendon. In others, such as in the muscle that runs up the front of the thigh, fascicles are arranged along both

These diagrams show various muscle shapes with examples:
- strap—helps movement of the head
- fusiform—raises lower arm
- unipennate—bends the thumb
- multipennate—raises the arm outward
- circular—controls lip movements

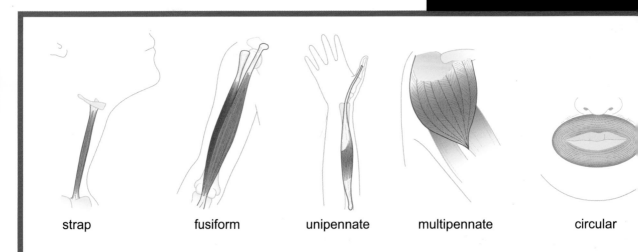

strap   fusiform   unipennate   multipennate   circular

sides of a central tendon. Muscles such as the powerful deltoid muscles of the shoulders, have fascicles that are attached at a range of angles to several tendons. Some muscles are triangular, with fascicles that fan out from a single central tendon. This arrangement forms powerful muscles, such as the pectoral muscles of the chest. Some muscles are circular, with fascicles arranged in concentric, or ever-widening, circles. These rings of muscle are called **sphincters**. They control the size of an opening, such as in the iris of the eye.

Muscle names

Although the names of muscles can seem complicated, they tell a lot about the muscle itself. Understanding muscle names is a little like cracking a code. When you know what each part of the name means, the meaning of the whole name is much easier to understand.

Naming muscles according to their action

An important characteristic of a muscle is the action it produces in the body. Muscles can be named according to these actions. Here are some examples:

- flexor—pulls two bones closer
- tensor—makes a body part tense or rigid
- rotator—rotates a body part
- extensor—extends a body part

Naming muscles according to their size

Muscles vary greatly in size. They can be named to give some idea of how big or small they are. Here are some examples:

- maximus—big
- minimus—small
- longus—long
- brevis—short

Naming muscles according to their position

Muscle names can give information about the position of a muscle in the body. For example:

- anterior—at the front
- posterior—at the back
- medial—in the middle

An example of a full muscle name is *extensor digitorum longus.*

extend   digits (toes)   long

When you break down the name like this, you can figure out that it is a long muscle that extends the toes.

Muscles are made up of separate strands, or **fibers**, bundled together and surrounded by layers of **membranes**. Blood vessels carry oxygen and other **nutrients** to the muscle and carry waste products away from it. Nerves carry signals from the brain to tell the muscles to contract.

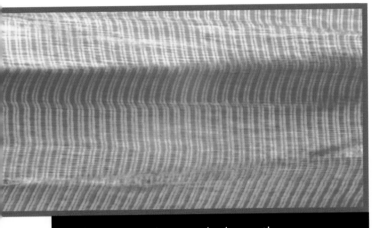

This photomicrograph shows the striated, or striped, pattern of skeletal muscle. The pattern is made by overlapping myofilaments.

Skeletal muscle

A skeletal muscle is surrounded and protected by an outer layer called the **epimysium**. Within this layer, individual muscle fibers are bound together into bundles called **fascicles**. In turn, each fascicle is surrounded by a protective layer, and the spaces between fascicles are filled with connective tissue. This tissue contains **capillaries,** which supply the individual fibers with nutrients and oxygen and remove waste products.

A fascicle can contain from 10 to 100 muscle fibers. Each fiber within a fascicle is surrounded by its own outer layer, called the **sarcolemma.** A muscle fiber is one elongated single cell, containing tiny threads called **myofibrils.** These extend the full length of the muscle fiber.

In turn, each myofibril is made up of even smaller structures called **myofilaments.** These do not extend the full length of the muscle fiber. Instead they are arranged one after another in a line, like separate cars that are linked together to make a complete train. The compartments, called sarcomeres, are separated from each other at either end by narrow plates called Z disks.

Different myofilaments

There are two types of myofilament: thick and thin. Each is made from different **proteins.** The thick myofilaments are largely made up of **myosin,** and the thin myofilaments are largely made up of **actin.** There are twice as many thin myofilaments as thick myofilaments. The thin filaments are attached to the Z disk, and the thick filaments are sandwiched between them. When the muscle contracts, the thick and thin myofilaments overlap, and when the muscle relaxes, they slide apart.

It is the overlapping of the thick and thin myofilaments that gives the muscle its **striated** appearance. Light patches appear where there are thin myofilaments alone, and dark patches appear where the thick and thin myofilaments overlap.

Motor neurons

Motor neurons carry signals from the brain to the muscle. They are linked to each muscle fiber. The neuron connects with a point on the muscle fiber wall called a **motor end plate**, which contains receptors for a chemical called **acetylcholine.**

Cardiac muscle

The smallest elements of **cardiac muscle** are thick and thin myofilaments, just as in skeletal muscle. The myofilaments overlap, creating a striated pattern similar to that of skeletal muscle. However, the fibers of cardiac muscle are cylindrical and are joined to neighboring fibers to form a branching network.

This diagram shows the structure of a skeletal muscle.

- The epimysium surrounds the entire muscle.
- Muscle fibers are bound together to form fascicles.
- Myofibrils are bound together to form muscle fibers.
- Myofibrils are made from overlapping myofilaments.

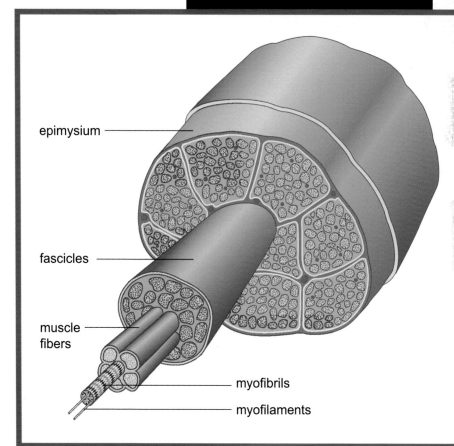

epimysium

fascicles

muscle fibers

myofibrils

myofilaments

Smooth muscle
Smooth muscle is also made up of thick and thin myofilaments. They are not arranged as regularly as those in skeletal and cardiac muscle, so there are no striations. Muscle fibers of smooth muscle are much smaller than those of skeletal muscle. In some smooth muscles, the fibers are linked to each other, while in other smooth muscles, the fibers are completely independent of each other.

MUSCLE ATTACHMENTS

Muscles allow you to move by pulling your bones. To do this, they have to be attached to bones.

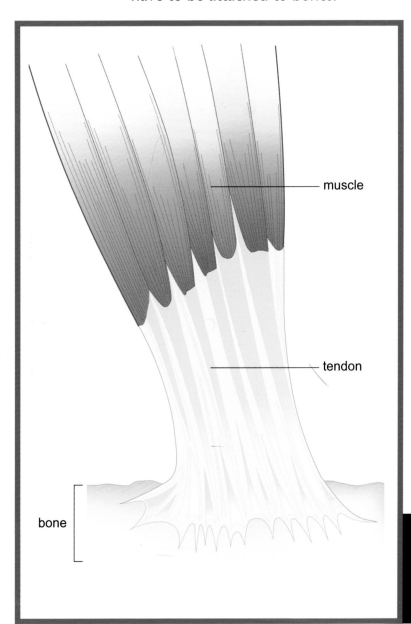

muscle

tendon

bone

Most muscles are attached to a bone by a strong cord called a **tendon**. Tendons are made from the fusing together of membranes that surround the **fascicles** of the muscle. Tendons extend into the outer covering of the bone, and some even extend into the outer layer of the bone itself. Tendons make a muscle longer by extending from each end of the muscle. They also reduce strain on the muscle itself.

The thickest tendon in the human body is the calcaneal tendon, usually known as the Achilles tendon. It attaches the calf muscle to the heel bone.

This diagram shows how a muscle may be attached to a bone.

Other attachments

Not all muscles are attached by cordlike tendons. In the abdominal wall, the tendon is spread out into a flat sheet, which is attached to the muscles lying beneath it. Many muscles in the face are attached directly to skin, which allows us to change our facial expression by pulling the skin into new positions.

Tendon problems

There are several common problems associated with tendons:

- Tendinitis. This occurs most often in the shoulder, heel, or hamstring, which is the muscle at the back of the thigh. This is a painful inflammation of a tendon or its surrounding membrane. It is often the result of a sports injury or a strain on the tendon. A condition known as tennis elbow affects people who rotate their forearms a lot, particularly in racquet sports. The tendon **fibers** become inflamed at the attachment to the elbow joint.

- Impingement syndrome. This condition causes shoulder pain in people who use a repetitive, overhead action, as in swimming, basketball, and volleyball. The action repeatedly crushes a tendon between the upper arm bone and the shoulder blade, causing inflammation and pain. It can eventually result in a rotator cuff injury, where the tendon wears away and tears away from the bone. An operation is necessary to repair the damage.

- Deep cut. Tendons, especially in the hand or foot, wrist, or ankle—where they lie just below the surface—can be severed by a deep cut. Usually, the two ends can be successfully sewn back together, although full strength may not always be restored.

- Extreme tension. Overstretching or jerking can damage a tendon, because some of the fibers anchoring it to the bone get pulled away. It can be treated with ice, rest, and bandages for support if needed. Sometimes, a cast is used to minimize movement and allow the tendon to heal naturally. An operation to reinforce the damaged area with **carbon fibers** can give the tendon extra strength.

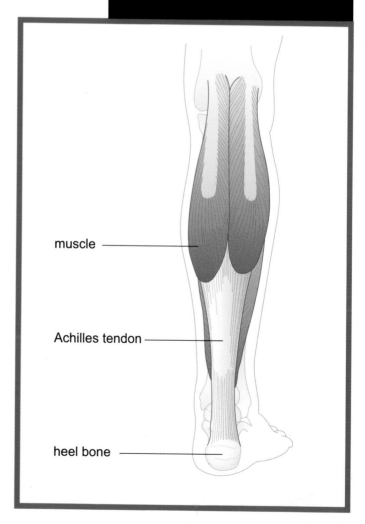

This diagram shows how the Achilles tendon links the calf muscle to the heel bone.

muscle

Achilles tendon

heel bone

WORKING MUSCLES

Most skeletal muscles work in pairs. Each muscle in a pair does the opposite job of the other muscle. When one muscle of a pair contracts, it stretches the other muscle, and vice versa.

Arm movement

The up and down movements of the lower arm are controlled by a pair of muscles. The biceps muscle is at the front of the upper arm and the triceps muscle is at the back. Both muscles are attached to the shoulder blade, the upper arm bone (humerus), and the lower arm bones.

When the biceps contracts, it pulls the lower arm bones up and stretches the triceps. When the triceps contracts, the opposite happens—the lower arm bones are pulled down and the biceps is stretched.

The same type of mechanism operates in many other movements, for example, when you nod your head up and down or raise and lower your leg. Two muscles that work together in this way are called an antagonistic pair.

These diagrams show how the biceps and triceps muscles work together to raise and lower the arm.

- The biceps contracts, the arm is pulled up, and the triceps is stretched.
- The triceps contracts, the arm is pulled down, and the biceps is stretched.

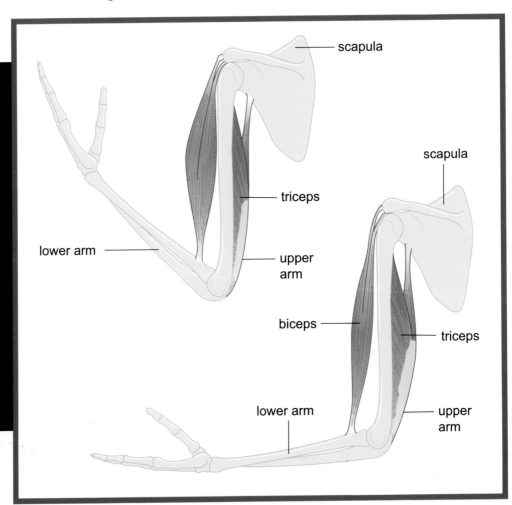

scapula

triceps

lower arm

upper arm

scapula

biceps

triceps

lower arm

upper arm

A system of levers

Muscle movements work in the same way as a system of levers. A lever arm (the bone) pivots around a fulcrum (the joint). Two forces act on the lever arm: the weight that has to be moved (the body or body part) and the pull of the muscle. There are three ways in which a lever system can work:

- First-class levers. These operate like a seesaw. The weight is at one end of the lever arm, the fulcrum is in the middle, and the force is at the other end. There are not many systems like this in the human body, but one is the head on the spine. When you lift your head, the weight that is to be moved is the back of your skull, the fulcrum is the joint between your skull and spine, and the lifting force is provided by your neck muscles.

- Second-class levers. These operate like a person pushing a wheelbarrow. The force is at one end of the lever arm, the fulcrum is at the other end, and the weight is in between. These systems do not allow fast, large movements, but they can provide a strong force. Again, these are not common in the human body. One example is when you raise yourself to stand on your tiptoes. The contraction of the calf muscles provides the lifting force, the ball of the foot acts as the fulcrum, and the body's weight pushes down in between.

- Third-class levers. These operate like a person lifting a weight on the end of a spade. The weight is at one end of the lever arm, the fulcrum is at the other end, and the force is in between. This is the most common system in the human body. It provides speed and a wide range of movement but little strength. Picking an object up in your hand uses this system. The object is the weight, the fulcrum is the elbow joint, and the lifting force is provided by the contraction of the biceps muscle.

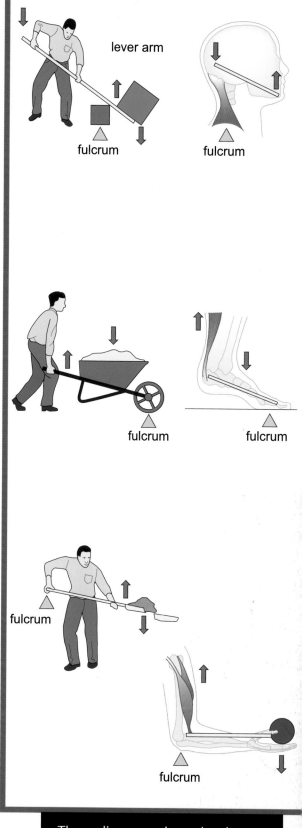

These diagrams show the three different lever systems.

WHEN A MUSCLE CONTRACTS

Skeletal muscles contract in response to a signal from the brain. The tiny **myofilaments** that make up the muscle **fibers** slide past each other, making the muscle shorter.

The contraction of a muscle is controlled by signals from the brain, which are carried to the muscle by nerves called **motor neurons.** Each neuron is linked to several muscle fibers. One motor neuron and all the muscle fibers it is linked to is called a **motor unit.** The fibers in a motor unit are usually spread evenly throughout a muscle. All the fibers in a motor unit receive the same signal, which makes them contract at the same time. The smallest signal that will make a motor unit contract is called its threshold stimulus.

All or nothing principle

The mechanism that controls muscle contractions operates on an all or nothing principle. If the signal is below the threshold, the motor unit will not respond and there will be no contraction. If the signal is greater than the threshold, the whole motor unit will contract. It does not make any difference if the signal is just a tiny amount bigger than the threshold or many times greater than the threshold, the response is exactly the same.

Small or large force?

Different motor units have different thresholds. Some respond to a much smaller stimulus than others. If the work to be done needs only a small force, a small signal from the brain stimulates just those motor units with a low threshold. If a more powerful force is required, the brain sends a stronger signal that stimulates more motor units. For the most powerful force, a very strong signal is sent, and all the motor units that make up the muscle are stimulated to contract.

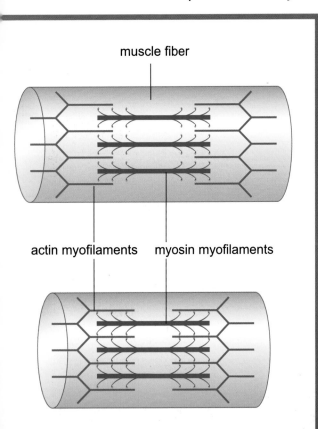

muscle fiber

actin myofilaments   myosin myofilaments

In the top diagram, the muscle fiber is relaxed. In the bottom diagram, the myosin filaments have slid past the actin filaments, making the muscle fiber shorter.

Motor end plates

The junction or space between a motor neuron and muscle fiber is called a **motor end plate**. When the neuron carries a signal to the motor end plate, a chemical is released, which stimulates the fibers to contract.

How does a muscle contract and relax?

A signal from the brain is carried by the motor neuron to the muscle fibers. The thick **myosin** myofilaments in the muscle move along the thin **actin** myofilaments, pulling them toward each other and making the muscle shorter. Chemical bridges form, holding the filaments in place.

The muscle fibers only contract for a short time and will relax unless they receive another signal from the brain telling them to maintain the contraction. When the muscle relaxes, the chemical bridges break down and the myosin myofilaments slide back past the actin myofilaments in the opposite direction, making the muscle longer.

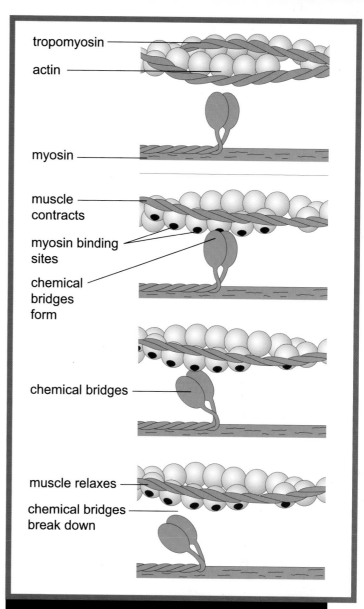

tropomyosin

actin

myosin

muscle contracts

myosin binding sites

chemical bridges form

chemical bridges

muscle relaxes

chemical bridges break down

These diagrams show how chemical bridges form when a muscle fiber contracts and break down when it relaxes.

Using energy

The muscle contraction process uses energy. The body stores energy that it gets from food. It is stored in a chemical called ATP. ATP can be changed into another chemical, ADP. When this happens, the stored energy is released. This process uses oxygen and produces water and carbon dioxide.

If there is not enough oxygen to change ATP into ADP, the muscles use a different process, called **anaerobic** respiration. This is much less efficient than **aerobic** respiration and can only be sustained for short periods.

ATHLETES' MUSCLES

Athletes train to make sure that their muscles are in prime condition. This enables them to attain their highest possible performance. There are differences between the muscles of different people, making them better suited to different activities.

Different types of muscle **fibers** contract at different rates. Fast-twitch fibers contract very quickly, while slow-twitch fibers contract more slowly. Different people may have different ratios of fast-twitch to slow-twitch fibers.

Slow-twitch fibers (Type I)

Slow-twitch fibers produce long, steady contractions and can maintain their effort for long periods of time without becoming **fatigued.** They have more **capillaries** than fast-twitch fibers have, giving them a red appearance, hence their name, red muscle. They also contain large amounts of myoglobin, a **protein** that can provide a small store of oxygen within the muscle. This ensures that there is a good supply of oxygen. Slow-twitch fibers use oxygen when they use stored energy. And their capillaries efficiently carry away waste products.

Fast-twitch fibers (Type II)

Fast-twitch fibers are good at producing short bursts of intense speed or force. They are often called white muscle because they contain relatively few blood capillaries, and therefore, they look pale. They also contain only small amounts of myoglobin. Fast-twitch fibers use stored energy without using oxygen. Waste products build up quickly, and the fibers soon become fatigued.

Long-distance runners need muscles that can work for long periods of time. Sprinters need muscles that provide short bursts of intense activity.

Different fibers for different activities

Fast-twitch and slow-twitch fibers are best suited to different types of activity. Fast-twitch fibers allow short, intense bursts of activity, such as sprinting very fast for a short distance, throwing a javelin a long way, or lifting heavy weights. Slow-twitch fibers are best for endurance activities such as long-distance running.

Changing the ratio

Some studies have suggested that, with appropriate training, it might be possible to increase the proportion of fast-twitch muscle fibers within a muscle, and thus increase the speed or strength of the muscle. However, research is still being carried out, and this has not yet been fully proved.

Athletes and drugs

Most people have heard about athletes being tested for drugs that enhance their performance. These include **anabolic steroids**, such as nandrolone, which increase the size and strength of muscles. However, these can have serious long-term side effects. Their use is banned in most competitive sports, and there are severe penalties for competitors found to have taken them.

These scientists are testing urine samples of athletes, checking for the presence of banned performance-enhancing drugs.

BODYBUILDING

Many people are not satisfied with the way their bodies look and want to change them in some way. Some want to have very strong, muscular bodies. They follow special diets and training programs to try to achieve this goal. In many cases, this does not cause a problem. However, using drugs and certain supplements to achieve this goal can be dangerous. Training with heavy weights at a young age can also be potentially harmful.

Bodybuilding is the name given to the process of increasing muscle mass and strength. To achieve this muscle development, people engage in intense training programs of weightlifting. Such programs concentrate on specific muscles and groups of muscles. In addition, bodybuilders may eat a **protein**-rich diet, which provides the nutritional building blocks for muscle development. Together, weight training and diet can help build muscle strength and size.

This bodybuilder demonstrates the strength and development of his muscles.

Teenage years

Many teenagers wish they could be stronger and more athletic. Often they also want to look more attractive. Although teenagers may be tempted to to improve their bodies by lifting weights, it is not a good idea to do so until they are older. Lifting heavy weights before the muscles are fully developed can cause muscle injuries. Weightlifting also puts pressure on the bones and, although this helps build bone in adults, it can inhibit bone growth in developing teenagers.

Superman!

Some bodybuilders are very proud of their achievements and enter competitions where they stand in different positions to display the size of specific muscle groups. One of the most famous bodybuilders was Charles Atlas, an Italian who emigrated to the United States. He developed a method of increasing muscle mass, called Dynamic Tension, and used it to transform his weak body into a stronger one. He won competitions and became a model for famous artists and sculptors. By selling his method to other people, he became very rich and successful.

Weight training can help to build muscle mass and increase strength.

The best way to ensure that your body grows healthy and strong is to take part in many physical activities. A variety of activities will help you improve your dexterity and coordination and increase your speed and strength. A balanced diet and plenty of rest are also important. All these factors will help your body develop healthily and naturally without any unnecessary pressure and strain.

Drugs

Anabolic steroids are human-made substances related to male **hormones.** There are some medical conditions which they can help, and they may be prescribed by a doctor. However, they are used by some people to help build muscle mass and strength. They can be taken by mouth or injected into the skin and are usually taken over weeks or months. Although they may have the desired effect on muscles, they can cause major side effects, including liver and kidney disease, high blood pressure, and mental disorders, such as mood swings and depression. Men who take anabolic steroids may suffer from over-aggression, infertility (problems conceiving babies), and baldness. Women who take them may become more masculine. They may grow facial hair, develop a deeper voice, and become infertile due to disruption of the menstrual cycle. For teenagers, anabolic steroids can prematurely stop their growth.

Creatine supplements

Creatine is a chemical made by the body and is also found in food. Adults need about two grams of creatine every day. It is required for the storage of energy in the muscles. In recent years, creatine supplements have become available, and some studies have suggested that these supplements can help to increase muscle mass and strength. However, other studies have shown that taking creatine supplements actually turns off the body's own production of creatine. The long-term effects are not yet known.

Cramp

Most people have experienced the sudden, sharp pain of a cramp. Cramps occur when a single muscle in a group of muscles suddenly contracts. The contraction may be over in a few seconds or may last several minutes. It happens most frequently in the leg or foot, often while exercising or when lying in bed. Cramps may occur for a variety of different reasons. Several factors seem to increase the risk, including low level of fitness, dehydration, lack of certain **minerals,** poor blood circulation in the legs, and wearing high-heeled shoes.

The pain of a cramp can usually be eased by stretching and gently massaging the affected muscle to stimulate blood circulation. Eating a balanced diet that contains plenty of fruit and vegetables reduces the likelihood of **vitamin** and mineral deficiency, and drinking plenty of water prevents dehydration. Wearing comfortable shoes with good arch support can also help prevent cramps from occurring. In some cases, a doctor may prescribe quinine to reduce the risk of cramps.

Tic

A tic is a repetitive, rapid, and involuntary contraction of a muscle. It usually involves muscles of the face and head and leads to exaggeration of normal movements, such as blinking or nodding.

Tics usually begin in children between the ages of nine and twelve, and they are more common in boys than girls. Most tics last less than one year—some last longer and others may last a lifetime. The reasons why tics develop are not clear, but they are often associated with stress and anxiety and get worse with strong emotions such as anger.

In most cases, tics simply disappear without treatment. In some severe cases, such as Tourette's syndrome, in which a child may have many tics and a lack of coordination, medication can help control the tic.

Sprains and strains

These two types of injuries are often confused because they produce similar symptoms. A sprain is an injury to the **ligaments,** the strong cords that bind together a joint. A strain is an injury to a muscle or **tendon.** Both can be caused by sudden movements, awkward falls, or unaccustomed exercise. They cause local pain, swelling, and restricted movement of the injured area.

Sprains and strains are usually treated with rest, ice to reduce swelling, and a bandage for support until the injury has healed. Painkillers can be taken to take away any immediate pain.

Aging and muscles

From around the age of 30, the amount of skeletal muscle in the body gradually reduces. Fibrous tissue and fatty tissue replace it. Muscle strength and the speed of reflexes also decrease with age. These changes take place partly because people tend to become less active as they get older. They can be stopped and even reversed if older people undertake endurance and strength training.

Rigor mortis

Most people are aware that after death the body becomes stiff with rigor mortis. This happens because **myosin myofilaments** bind to **actin** myofilaments. They cannot detach themselves again, and so the muscles cannot contract or relax. It begins within a few hours of death and can last up to 24 hours. The stiffness disappears as the **protein** molecules in the muscles break down.

This athlete is suffering from a cramp in his thigh muscle. Gentle massage can help relieve the problem.

MUSCLES OF THE FACE AND HEAD

The muscles of the head and neck hold the head in position and allow it to move. The human face can show many different expressions, such as smiling and frowning. These are possible because there is a network of more than 30 muscles that work together to move its different parts. These muscles are also important in chewing food and producing the sounds of speech.

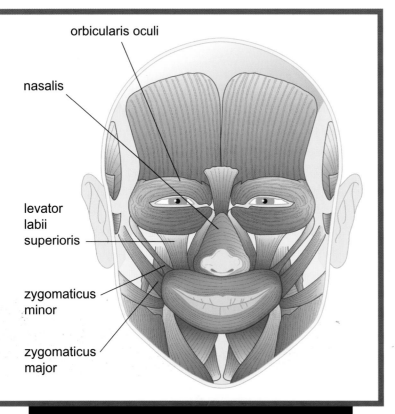

orbicularis oculi

nasalis

levator labii superioris

zygomaticus minor

zygomaticus major

This diagram shows the main muscles used when a person smiles.

The head is balanced on top of the spine. Pairs of muscles contract to allow you to nod your head up and down, and other pairs contract to allow you to rotate it from side to side. Strong muscles in the neck hold the head in its usual upright position.

Facial expressions

The muscles that control facial expressions are not just in the face but also in the scalp and neck. They are attached to skin, bones, and **tendons**.

Around the eyes, nose, and mouth, rings of circular muscle called **sphincters** control the openings.

The tongue

The muscles of the tongue allow you to fold, curve, and squeeze the tongue. They also allow you to poke it out and in, up and down. These tongue muscles are essential for eating and normal speech, but they can cause problems when a person is unconscious. The tongue can move backward and block the airway, preventing normal breathing. This is often referred to as swallowing one's tongue. When administering first aid to an unconscious person, it is important to check that this has not happened. When a **general anesthetic** is administered to a patient in hospital, a narrow tube is inserted into the mouth to keep the airway open.

When we smile, the corners of the upper lip are lifted as muscles in the angles of the mouth contract. When we frown, other muscles pull down the corners of the mouth, wrinkle the forehead, and lower the eyelids. Smiling uses only 17 muscles, whereas frowning uses 43!

Muscles in the sides of the cheeks move food around inside the mouth as we chew. These muscles are also important when we blow or suck. Some jazz trumpeters overuse these cheek muscles so much so that they lose their elasticity and automatically balloon outward whenever the trumpeter begins to play.

Other muscles raise and lower the bottom jaw so that we can chew and speak.

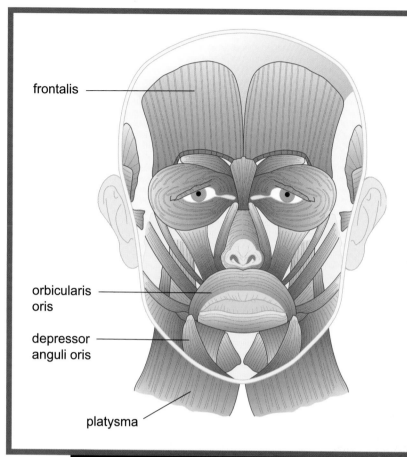

frontalis

orbicularis oris

depressor anguli oris

platysma

This diagram shows the main muscles used when a person frowns.

Problems

Some other problems can occur with the muscles of the face and head:

- Headache. Tension headaches are most often caused by stress and tiredness. Painful contractions of muscles at the back of the neck and head cause discomfort, and pain spreads from the back of the head toward the eyes. The headache can get worse as blood vessels in the scalp constrict, reducing the blood supply and allowing waste products to build up. Tension headaches can often be eased by sleep or by taking painkillers.
- Bell's palsy. This is a one-sided paralysis of the face, due to damage to a facial nerve. Its cause is unknown, but in some cases, it may be triggered by extreme cold. Because of nerve damage, signals from the brain cannot reach the facial muscles. This means that the whole of one side of the face droops, so that the person cannot wrinkle the forehead, close the eye, or pucker the lips, and he or she may have difficulty swallowing. The problem can be permanent, but most people recover fully in a few weeks.

THE CHEST MUSCLES

The structure and shape of the chest is formed by the thoracic bones of the spine, the ribs and the sternum (breastbone). The muscles attached to these bones allow us to breathe. Some also help upper body movements and some help with abdominal functions.

Breathing

When we breathe, we use several groups of muscles.

- External intercostal muscles are attached to the bottom of one rib and to the top of the rib below. When they contract, all the ribs are lifted upward and outward.
- Internal intercostal muscles are also attached to the bottom of one rib and to the top of the rib below, but they run at a different angle to the external intercostal muscles. When these contract, all the ribs are forced downward and inward.
- The diaphragm is a large, dome-shaped sheet of muscle surrounding a central **tendon.** It forms a partition between the chest and the abdomen. When the diaphragm contracts, it flattens and moves downward. When it relaxes, it moves upward and regains its dome-shape.

Breathing in and out

- Breathing in: Together, the contraction of the diaphragm and external intercostal muscles increases the space inside the rib cage, and air is sucked into the lungs.
- Breathing out: When the diaphragm relaxes and the internal intercostal muscles contract, the space inside the rib cage decreases, and air is forced out of the lungs.

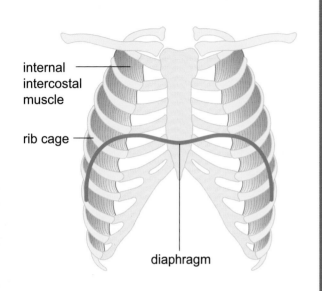

internal intercostal muscle

rib cage

diaphragm

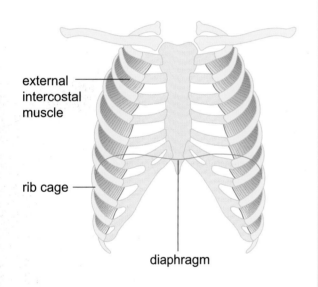

external intercostal muscle

rib cage

diaphragm

These diagrams show how the chest muscles help us to breathe in and out.
- Breathing in: The external intercostal muscles and diaphragm contract to increase space inside the rib cage (top).
- Breathing out: Internal intercostal muscles contract and the diaphragm relaxes to decrease the space inside the rib cage (bottom).

Diaphragm

The diaphragm has important functions besides its role in breathing. When it contracts and moves downward, it pushes on the organs of the abdomen and increases the pressure inside the abdomen. This can help to push waste out of the rectum and urine out of the bladder. The diaphragm can also help in childbirth, by forcing the baby out of the mother's body. When we lift heavy weights, we rely on the extra downward pressure that the diaphragm can exert.

Opera singers are trained to use their diaphragms to help them to exert very precise control over their breathing.

Problems with chest muscles

Some problems can occur with the chest muscles, including the following:

- Stitch: When you run, the diaphragm may become short of oxygen and waste products may build up. You feel a sharp pain in your side called a stitch, as the diaphragm becomes **fatigued**. After a short rest, the pain goes away, and you can continue running.

- Hiccup: Most people have suffered from hiccups at some time. They happen when the regular, rhythmic contractions of the diaphragm become short, irregular, and uncontrollable. This is what causes the short, sharp intakes of breath called hiccups.

- Paralysis: This occurs when damage to nerves prevents signals from the brain from reaching muscles. The muscles therefore do not contract and relax. Paralysis of the chest muscles makes breathing impossible. This can occur as the result of an accident or an infection, for example, polio. A heart-lung machine can take over and breathe artificially to keep the patient alive.

- Anesthetic: When a patient is given a **general anesthetic,** he or she is usually given a muscle relaxant drug as well. This relaxes all the muscles and makes surgery easier. It also makes it impossible for the patient to breathe, because the chest muscles cannot contract. The anesthesiologist controls the patient's oxygen levels using a breathing machine called a ventilator. When the operation is over, another drug is given to reverse the effects of the muscle relaxant. Then the patient is able to breathe normally again.

THE HEART MUSCLE

The heart is made up of **cardiac muscle**. This special **involuntary muscle** contracts regularly and continually throughout your life, ensuring that blood circulates to every part of your body. The heart beats roughly 70 times every minute, 100,000 times every day, 35 million times a year. If you live to be 70 years old, your heart will have beaten 2.5 billion times!

This photo-micrograph shows the internal structure of cardiac muscle. The tissue is **striated**, similar to skeletal muscle, but the fibers are interlinked, rather than parallel.

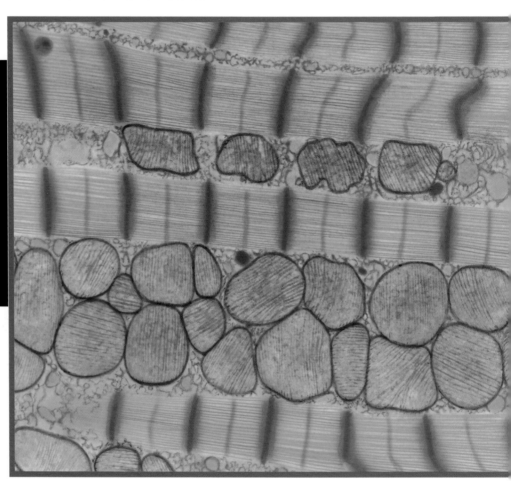

Cardiac muscle

Cardiac muscle is found only in the heart. It is made up of the same **myofibril** and **protein** components as skeletal muscle, but the muscle **fibers** are organized in a different way. In skeletal muscle, the muscle fibers all run parallel to each other. They do not cross or join. In cardiac muscle, the fibers are branched and interlinked, forming a thick network of muscle tissue.

The contraction of cardiac muscle is partly regulated by nerve signals. But cardiac muscle is also able to contract rhythmically without these signals. Muscle fibers are coordinated to contract so that the movements of the heart chambers follow a certain order at all times and blood is pumped efficiently.

Heart attack

Cardiac muscle uses oxygen to release energy, converting ATP to ADP (see page 21). To maintain its contractions, therefore, it needs a good supply of oxygen. Coronary arteries bring blood to the heart muscle, supplying it with **nutrients** and oxygen and removing waste products. If the coronary arteries become blocked, and the blood supply is interrupted, the contractions of the heart muscle become irregular and may stop altogether. This is a heart attack.

The contraction of muscle fibers can become irregular and lose their coordination. This causes weak twitching, called fibrillation, instead of strong contractions. The heart chambers cannot contract properly, so blood is not pumped efficiently, which may result in death. Rhythm disturbances can often be treated with drugs. A device called a defibrillator can be used to give an electric shock, which stimulates the muscle fibers to become coordinated once again.

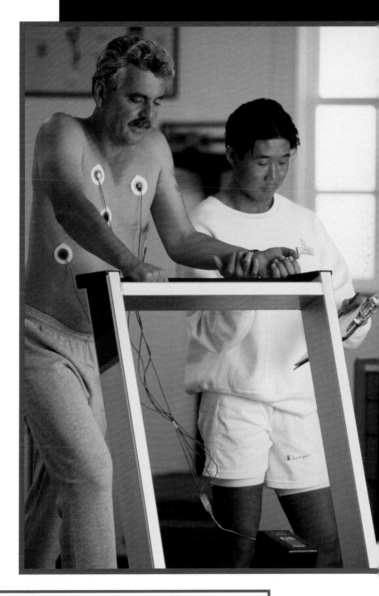

This patient's heartbeat is being monitored as he exercises. This helps doctors assess how efficiently his heart is working.

Look after your heart

Like all muscles, the more you use the heart muscle, the stronger it becomes. Regular **aerobic** exercise can help keep the heart in excellent condition and reduce the risk of heart disease in later life.

Alcohol and smoking can both lead to heart problems, so it makes sense to avoid them. Being very overweight puts an extra strain on the heart, while being underweight can lead to the breakdown of the heart muscle. A well-balanced diet and exercise play important roles in maintaining a healthy body weight and, thus, a healthy heart.

The wall of the abdomen contains many muscles arranged in layers. They control movements of the skeleton and maintain posture and balance. They are also involved with assisting the functions of some internal organs.

Abdominal wall

The abdominal wall supports and protects the internal organs of the abdomen. A strong **tendon,** the linea alba, runs down the midline of the body, from the sternum to the front of the pelvis, or pubic bone. Four layers of muscle are built around this tendon, offering support around the abdomen. The outermost layer is the external abdominal oblique muscle. **Fibers** run forward and downward from the ribs and are attached to the linea alba in the center. The next layer is the internal abdominal oblique muscle. Fibers run forward and upward from each side of the pelvis to the linea alba. Below these muscles is the transverse abdominis muscle. It runs horizontally from the spine to the linea alba. The innermost layer of the abdominal wall is the rectus abdominis muscle. It runs vertically from the ribs to the pubic bone.

The contraction of muscles of the abdominal wall increases the pressure within the abdomen and on the abdominal organs. This is important in urination, **defecation,** and childbirth.

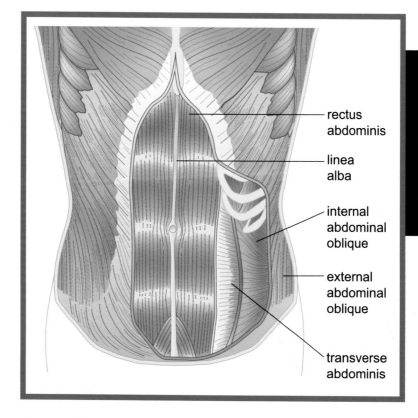

rectus abdominis

linea alba

internal abdominal oblique

external abdominal oblique

transverse abdominis

The abdominal wall is made up of four strong muscle layers and the linea alba tendon.

Hernia

A hernia occurs when an area of the abdominal wall becomes weak. Part of the small intestine may stick out through some or all of the layers of the wall, causing a lump. Hernias usually occur near the groin, called inguinal hernia, or near the navel, called umbilical hernia. Hernias are more common in men than in women. Some people are born with a weakness that makes it likely they will develop a hernia. In other cases, hernias can be caused by a serious, persistent cough that causes high pressure within the abdomen, or by heavy lifting. Hernias can be repaired surgically.

Pelvic muscles

There are two main groups of pelvic muscles. They make up the pelvic diaphragm and the perineum. Together, these form the floor of the pelvis, supporting the pelvic organs. They help to maintain the internal abdominal pressure and control defecation and urination. They are also important in childbirth.

Lower back muscles

On each side at the back of the body, a strong muscle, the quadratus lumborum, is attached to the pelvis, the **lumbar vertebrae**, and the twelfth rib. The contraction of these muscles results in side-to-side movements of the body. Also, together these muscles help provide stability.

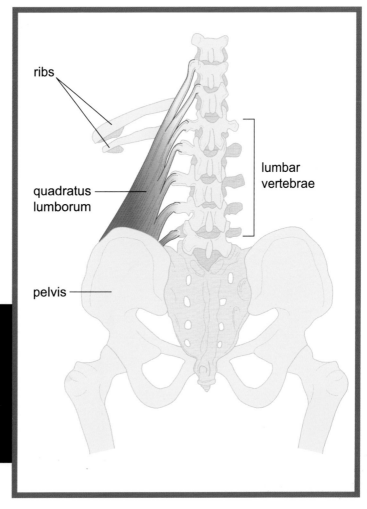

ribs

quadratus lumborum

lumbar vertebrae

pelvis

The quadratus lumborum muscle allows side-to-side movements and provides stability.

INTERNAL INVOLUNTARY MUSCLES

Some internal organs and vessels contain **involuntary muscles**. These **smooth muscles** are involved in internal processes essential to the normal functioning of the body.

Digestive system

The alimentary canal is a long tube that makes up most of the digestive system. Although there are variations in its size and surface detail, the basic structure is the same throughout its length:

- The outer layer is a thin layer of connective tissue.
- Beneath this is a layer of muscle **fibers,** which run along the length of the wall.
- Next comes a layer of circular muscle fibers, which run in rings around the wall.
- Below this is a thick layer of connective tissue, which contains nerves and blood vessels.
- The innermost layer produces **mucus** that keeps food slippery, helping it to slide easily along.
- At the center is the lumen, the space through which food moves. The muscle fibers in the wall of the alimentary canal contract regularly, creating a rippling wavelike movement called peristalsis. This movement pushes food along the canal.

esophagus

liver

stomach

pancreas

duodenum

colon

The walls of the alimentary canal contain smooth muscles that contract to push the food along.

Blood vessels

Blood vessels carry blood from the heart, around the body, and back to the heart again. The heart pumps blood out at great pressure. This means that the vessels that carry blood away from the heart have to be very strong to withstand the force. The arteries have strong walls made up of three layers:

- a thick outer layer of collagen fibers
- a thick middle layer of elastic and muscle fibers arranged in rings
- a thin lining layer.

The walls of major arteries are elastic. This allows them to stretch as the heart pumps blood into them.

Veins carry blood back to the heart. They have thinner walls than arteries have, because they carry blood at a lower pressure. Their walls also have three layers:

- a thin outer layer of collagen fibers
- a thin middle layer, containing few muscle fibers
- a thin lining layer.

Goosebumps

Smooth muscles, each called an arrector pili, are attached to the dermis of the skin and to the side of each hair follicle. When these muscles are relaxed, the hairs leave the skin at a fairly shallow angle and lay flat. When the muscles contract, the hairs are pulled up straight and stand upright. This often happens when you are cold or scared, and you usually refer to the effect as goosebumps.

Airways

The bronchioles are narrow passages within the lungs. Their walls contain rings of smooth muscle, forming spiral bands. The bronchioles do not contain any supporting material. If the muscles contract, the airways can narrow and close. This happens in an asthma attack. An **allergic reaction** leads to the contraction of these muscles, causing breathing difficulties. Special drugs can be taken, usually with an inhaler, to prevent spasms of the bronchiole muscles.

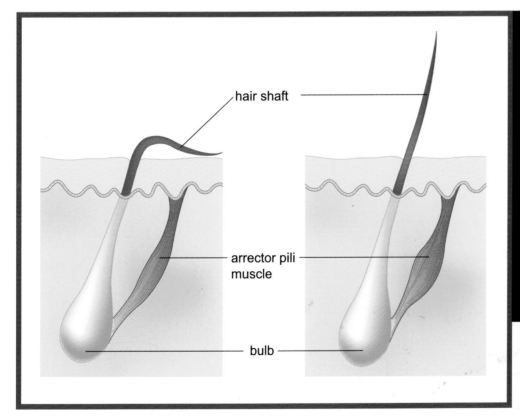

hair shaft

arrector pili muscle

bulb

In the picture on the left, the muscle is relaxed and the hair is lying flat. In the picture on the right, the muscle has contracted and pulled the hair upright.

ARM AND HAND MUSCLES

The muscles that move the bones of the arm and hand allow a wide range of movements. You can throw a ball with great strength using the full power of the shoulder, and you can make tiny, precise movements with each finger.

Moving the upper arm

Several groups of muscles control the movement of the shoulder joint. The four rotator cuff **tendons** are attached to the shoulder blade (scapula) and the upper arm bone (humerus). These tendons help prevent dislocation and instability. The deltoid muscles form the rounded shape of the shoulder and are attached to the scapula, humerus, and collarbone (clavicle). The pectoral muscles of the chest are attached to the clavicle, sternum, ribs, and humerus. Together, these muscles move the shoulder joint in three directions: up and down, side to side, and backward and forward. This allows for complete rotation and circular movements. The muscles are powerful, which allows the upper arm to exert great force.

Moving the lower arm

The arm is hinged at the elbow, allowing the lower arm to be flexed or extended, or raised and lowered. Two muscles control this movement. The biceps contracts to raise the lower arm, and the triceps contracts to lower the arm. This movement is described in greater detail on page 18.

This diagram shows some of the major muscles that move the shoulder and upper arm.

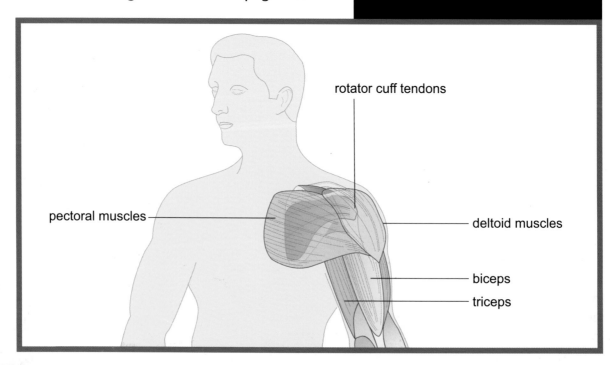

rotator cuff tendons

pectoral muscles

deltoid muscles

biceps

triceps

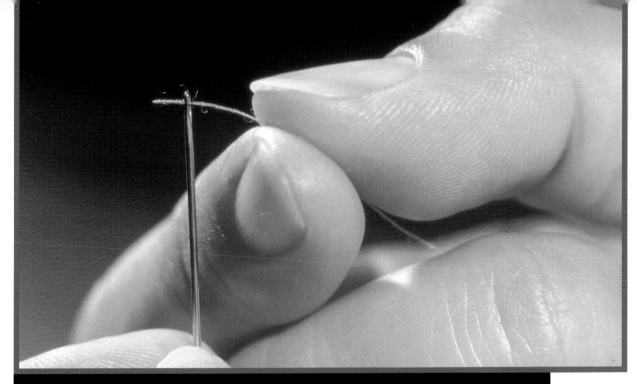

The human hand is capable of carrying out very tiny, precise movements.

Moving the wrist

The complex wrist joints allow you to lift your hand up and down and move it from side to side. You can also rotate it so that the palm faces up or down. Many different muscles are involved in moving the wrist. They are attached to the humerus and lower arm bones and to the carpal bones of the wrist.

Moving the hand

The fingers are hinged so you can move them up and down, as well as bend them at each individual joint. Each finger and thumb is controlled by the contraction of its own individual muscles. Muscles of the palm and back of the hand allow you to spread the fingers apart.

The human thumb is capable of a special movement called opposition, meaning that the thumb can be brought across the palm of the hand to touch the little finger. This movement is found only in humans and some other primates. It allows you to grasp objects with great precision.

Carpal tunnel syndrome

The carpal tunnel is a narrow channel in the wrist through which nerves and tendons pass. Sometimes, these nerves and tendons can get squashed, causing pain and weakness in the hand. This is called carpal tunnel syndrome. It can be a result of injury or infection but is more often due to excessive repetitive exercises, such as playing the piano or using a computer keyboard or typewriter. Usually, the symptoms can be cured simply by resting and avoiding the exercise that caused the problem in the first place. However, surgery is sometimes necessary.

LEG AND FOOT MUSCLES

The muscles that control the movement of the hip joint are the largest and most powerful in the body. They provide stability for the joint and power to move the whole body. The muscles of the legs and feet also allow you to stand upright. They help you maintain your posture and, by operating in sequence, allow you to walk and run.

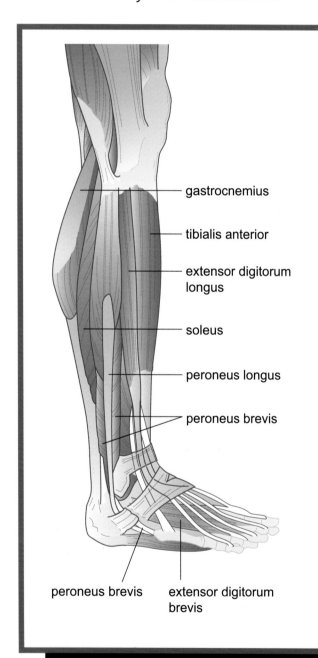

gastrocnemius

tibialis anterior

extensor digitorum longus

soleus

peroneus longus

peroneus brevis

peroneus brevis

extensor digitorum brevis

This diagram shows some of the major muscles that move the leg and foot.

Moving the thigh

The hip joint is a strong ball-and-socket joint. It allows the thigh to move in a wide variety of ways. Strong muscles surround the joint to provide stability and prevent dislocation. The gluteus maximus muscle is used when powerful movements are needed, such as when climbing stairs, running, and jumping.

Moving the lower leg

When the hamstring muscles at the back of the thigh contract, the lower leg is pulled back. When muscles at the front of the thigh contract, the lower leg is pulled forward.

Moving the foot

When muscles at the back of the lower leg contract, the heel is raised. When muscles at the front of the lower leg contract, the ball of the foot and toes are raised. Several muscles work together to allow the foot to rotate freely at the ankle joint. Within the foot, strong muscles contract to maintain the arch of the foot and allow it to flex as you walk. Individual muscles move each toe in a manner similar to the muscles in the hand that move the fingers. However, unlike the toes of some other primates, the big toe operates exactly as the other toes do and cannot move in opposition as the thumb can.

When you walk, the muscles of the leg and foot operate in a precise sequence.

Common injuries

Because you use the muscles of the legs and feet so much, they are prone to injury, especially when you engage in sports. Some common injuries include:

- Groin strain. This is the most common injury in activities that involve quick sprints, such as soccer, tennis, and running. Muscles deep in the groin may be stretched or torn, causing pain. With rest and **physical therapy,** the injury usually heals completely.

- Pulled hamstring. The hamstring is one of the strong muscles at the back of the thigh. It may be strained or partially torn by running very hard or by an abrupt start or stop. There is usually bruising and intense pain. The risk of hamstring injury can be reduced by proper training and adequate stretching exercises before and after any activity.

- Shinsplints. Tendinitis, or inflammation of a **tendon,** causes pain along the length of the shin bones. This is usually the result of running on hard surfaces in poor shoes, or it occurs after a sudden burst of intense exercise after a long period of inactivity.

- Plantar fasciitis. Also called painful heel syndrome, this is the most common cause of heel pain in runners. It is usually due to the repeated impact of the foot on the ground, causing inflammation of the muscle that attaches to the heel bone.

Achilles injury

The Achilles tendon can be injured in several ways. The injury can be at the point where the tendon is attached to the heel bone or just above the heel bone. Strains, minor tears, and inflammations cause pain that may develop slowly or appear suddenly. The pain is usually worse when the tendon is stretched, such as when running uphill.

Minor injuries can be caused by poor sports shoes, so it is important to check that your shoes fit well and that there is no friction between the shoes and the back of your ankle.

Treatment for an injured Achilles tendon depends on the extent of the injury. X rays may be needed to check that there is no damage to the heel bone. For minor injuries, an injection may be given to reduce inflammation. Rest, heat treatment, and ultrasound all help accelerate the healing process.

Motor neuron disease

Motor neuron disease is not a disease of the muscles themselves, but it prevents muscle contraction. Muscles can contract only in response to a signal from the brain. These signals are carried along nerves called motor neurons. In motor neuron disease, the neurons slowly break down and waste away. At first, it may cause only minor difficulties, such as weakness and stiffness. Slowly, it affects more muscles and difficulties become greater, affecting functions such as speech and swallowing. The cause of motor neuron disease is unknown, and there is no effective long-term treatment. In some people, it is fatal in a short period of time. Others, such as physicist Stephen Hawking, can live for many years with the condition.

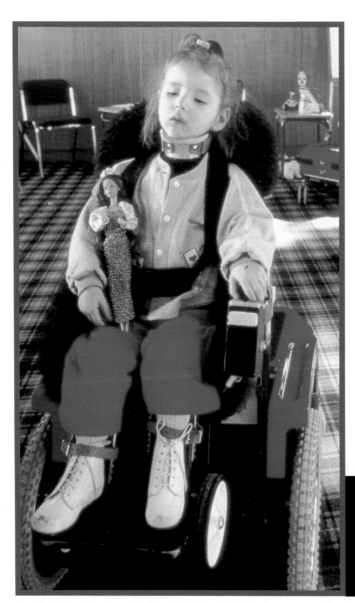

This girl has muscular dystrophy. Her weak muscles make walking difficult, and she relies on a wheelchair to get around.

Myasthenia gravis

Myasthenia gravis is much more common in women than in men and causes extreme fatigue. It is an autoimmune disease, which means that the immune system recognizes parts of the body as foreign and attacks them. The immune system produces chemicals called antibodies against the **acetylcholine** receptors of the muscle **fibers.** These antibodies bind to the receptors and block them. When acetylcholine is released, the receptors do not detect it, and therefore, the muscles do not contract. Some drug treatments can be given to increase the levels of acetylcholine in the body, and steroids can be given to prevent antibody production.

Muscular dystrophy

Muscular dystrophy is the name given to a group of inherited diseases, all of which cause muscle weakness. The most common, and most severe, is Duchenne's muscular dystrophy, which affects boys mostly. Initially, the muscles of the thigh and pelvis are weak, making it difficult to stand and walk. Later, other muscles become weak, affecting other movements. If the muscles involved in breathing or the heart muscle are affected, the patient may die. Treatment by exercise and **physical therapy** can help, but most people with the condition die at an early age.

Paralysis

Paralysis is not a disease of the muscles, but it is caused by the failure of signals from the brain to reach the muscles. Spinal injuries can cause paralysis, because damage to the spinal cord disrupts signals to and from the brain. If the injury is in the neck, all four limbs may be paralyzed and the patient is said to be quadraplegic or tetraplegic (*tetra* is the Greek word for four). A lower spinal injury may mean that the person can still move the arms, but the legs and lower body are paralyzed. He or she is said to be paraplegic. A stroke, or blood clot in the brain, can cause paralysis. Usually, this affects only one side of the body and may be temporary.

Spinal cord injuries can result in paralysis. Christopher Reeve, who starred as the film hero "Superman," suffered a serious spinal cord injury when he fell from his horse.

Technological solutions?

Scientists are working on many different ideas to try to make life easier for people who are paralyzed. Some recent research has shown that monkeys can be trained to move the cursor on a computer screen by using just their brainpower. Electrodes connected to the monkeys' brains can pick up electrical signals from nerve cells. The signals are interpreted electronically, and the cursor moves in the direction the monkey wants it to. Scientists hope that one day people who are paralyzed will be able to control robotic arms and legs in a similar way.

WHAT CAN GO WRONG WITH THE MUSCLES?

This book has explained the different parts of the muscular system, why they are important, and how they can be damaged by injury and illness. This page summarizes some of the problems that can affect the muscles. It also gives information about how each problem can be treated.

Many problems can be avoided or prevented by maintaining a healthy lifestyle. Getting regular exercise and plenty of rest are important, as is eating a balanced diet. This is especially important in your teenage years, when your body is still developing. This table tells you some of the ways you can prevent muscle injury and illness.

Remember, if you think something is wrong with your body, talk to a trained medical professional such as a doctor or your school nurse. Regular medical checkups are an important part of maintaining a healthy body.

Illness or injury	Cause	Symptoms	Prevention	Treatment
tendinitis	inflammation of a **tendon** or its surrounding **membrane**	painful joint; may be swollen, with restriction of movement	avoid repetition of painful movement	rest; ice pack; anti-inflammatory drugs may be prescribed
extreme tension	damage to a tendon from overstretching or jerking	painful joint; may be swollen, with restriction of movement	maintain a healthy lifestyle; avoid overstretching or jerking muscles	rest; ice pack; support bandage; painkillers may be prescribed
cramp	sudden contraction of a group of muscles	sudden pain that lasts for a few seconds or longer	regular exercise; eat a healthy diet; drink plenty of water	gentle stretching and massage of affected muscles
sprain	injury to a **ligament** due to an awkward fall or unaccustomed exercise	swollen painful joint, with restriction of movement	maintain a healthy lifestyle; avoid sudden excessive movements	rest; ice pack; support bandage; painkillers may be prescribed
strain	injury to a muscle or tendon, often due to an awkward fall or unaccustomed exercise	swollen painful joint, with restriction of movement	maintain a healthy lifestyle; avoid sudden excessive movements	rest; ice pack; support bandage; painkillers may be prescribed

# FURTHER READING

Goode, Katherine. *Skeleton and Muscles.* Detroit, Mich:
Gale Group, 2000.

Lemley Burnett, Gail. *Muscular Dystrophy.* Berkeley Heights, N.J.:
Enslow, 2000.

Parker, Steve. *Muscles.* Brookfield, Conn.: Millbrook, 1997.

Saunderson, Jane. *Muscles and Bones.* Mahwah, N.J.: Troll
Communications, 1997.

Taylor, Barbara. *The Muscular System.* New York: Rosen, 2000.

acetylcholine chemical released by a nerve carrying a signal from the brain to a muscle

actin main protein of thin myofilaments

aerobic chemical reaction that uses oxygen

allergic reaction reaction by the body to an antigen to which it is sensitive. For example, people with hay fever have an allergic reaction to pollen in which their noses run and eyes become sore.

amino acid one of the basic units of a protein molecule

anabolic steroid human-made drug that increases muscle mass and strength

anaerobic chemical reaction that does not use oxygen

capillary delicate blood vessel that runs between veins and arteries

carbon fiber strong threads of carbon that can be woven into a very strong material

cardiac muscle muscle tissue of the heart

defecation removal of solid waste from the body

epimysium outer covering of a muscle

fascicle bundle of muscle fibers

fatigued describes a muscle that is tired due to the buildup of waste products

fiber single muscle cell

general anesthetic drug given to make a person sleep during a medical procedure to prevent them from feeling anything

hormone chemical made in the body that travels around the body in the blood and affects organs and tissues in a variety of ways

involuntary muscle muscle that contracts without conscious control

ligament strong cord that binds joints together

lumbar relating to the lower back

membrane thin covering layer of tissue

mineral chemical needed by the body in very small amounts, for example, calcium and iron

motor end plate junction between a motor neuron and a muscle fiber

motor neuron nerve that carries signals from the brain to muscle

motor unit motor neuron and all the muscle fibers it stimulates

mucus sticky, slimy fluid that acts as a lubricant

myofibril thin strand inside a muscle fiber

myofilament strand of protein inside a myofibril

myosin main protein of thick myofilaments

nutrient part of food that the body can use

physical therapy exercise and other treatments to help a person recover after injury

protein complex chemical that is a component of many of the body's structures

sarcolemma outer membrane covering of a muscle fiber

smooth muscle involuntary muscle of some internal organs and vessels

sphincter ringlike muscle that controls the size of an opening

striated striped

tendon strong fibrous cord that attaches muscle to bone

vertebra segment of the backbone

vitamin complex chemical that the body needs in very small amounts

voluntary muscle muscle that is under conscious control

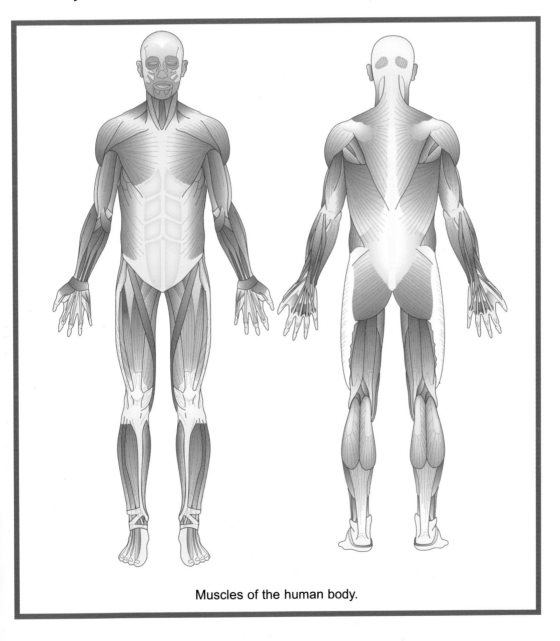

Muscles of the human body.

INDEX